A WOMEN'S MINISTRY GUIDE TO
Scrapbooking

A complete guide to establishing an outreach program in today's most meaningful hobby.

SANDRA L. JOSEPH

A WOMEN'S MINISTRY GUIDE TO
Scrapbooking
A complete guide to establishing
an outreach program in
today's most meaningful hobby.

by Sandra L. Joseph

Published by Reminders Of Faith, Inc.
518 Overhead Drive
Moon Township, PA 15108
orders@remindersoffaith.com
www.remindersoffaith.com

Copyright © Reminders of Faith, 2005
All rights reserved.

President: Sandra L. Joseph
Vice President: Kathy Brundage
Art Director: Beth Beiter
Editor: Tonja M. Brossette
Graphic Designer: Beth Beiter
Illustrator: Gina Hurst
Scrapbook Page Layout Artists:
Beth Beiter
Valerie DeFor
Corrine French

Paper Broker and Advisor: Nancy Guthrie
Photography by Paul Palermo, Palermo Imaging, Warrendale, PA
Photography by Sally Maxson, Beaver Falls, PA

Scripture taken from the HOLY BIBLE:
NEW INTERNATIONAL VERSION®.
NIV®. Copyright ©1973, 1978, 1984 by International Bible Society.
Used with permission of The Zondervan Corporation.

ISBN 0-9763691-6-8

Table of Contents

Letter to the Reader	4
What Makes Your Event a "Ministry"	6
How To Get Started: Scrapbooking	8
Planning Your Scrapbook Ministry Event	10
Planning and Executing a Crop	15
Teaching a Class on Scrapbooking Your Faith	23
Using Reminders of Faith Theme Packs at Your Scrapbook Ministry Event	26
Using Reminders of Faith *Remember the Wonders* kits at Your Scrapbook Ministry Event	28
Basic Scrapbook Information: How To Get Started, Terms and Techniques, etc.	31
Frequently Asked Questions	33
Other Paper Crafting Projects for Scrapbook Ministries	35
Contact Information	36
Our Mission	37
Product & Ordering Information	38

3

Since the late 1990's, scrapbooking has become an admired hobby in America. So popular, in fact, that over 25% of all American households will create some type of scrapbook throughout each year.

It is estimated that over 90% of scrapbooking enthusiasts are comprised of women, as this art carries many qualities in which women find enjoyment. They gain a sense of fulfillment from creating with their hands, coming together with other women to fellowship, and working on a craft that their families will cherish for generations to come. Most importantly, women find value in this important art of preserving memories. In Luke 2:19 we are told that Mary treasured memories in her heart, and this is precisely what women accomplish as they scrapbook – the preservation of treasured memories.

All of these facets of scrapbooking make it a wonderful fit for a women's ministry program. Utilizing the appeal and popularity of scrapbooking, women's ministries can design and implement events that reach out to others - not only in their churches, but also to those in their communities. As women gather to meet, they will develop relationships with one another, achieving the goal of enhancing and strengthening their individual Christian walks.

Another very exciting feature of a Scrapbooking Ministry is the way it appeals to the non-believer. Many non-believers are willing to come to a scrapbooking event at a church, even despite a disinterest in attending a church service. Women who come to a church event to scrapbook are also given the opportunity to learn of the programs offered by the church, and in turn, have the opportunity to learn of salvation through Christ.

As you make plans for a Scrapbooking Ministry in your church, this booklet will become an invaluable tool for you. Use it as a guide for ideas, promotions, themes, and basic scrapbooking information. We encourage you to surround your scrapbooking ministry in prayer; pray for every aspect of this ministry, the promotion, the women who will attend, the atmosphere of the room, the fellowship created, and for God's stories to be told through the pages of their creations. Pray for believers as well as non-believers to attend. And pray that the scrapbook pages created would share God's faithfulness among the attendees and their generations to come.

I believe that God will use your scrapbooking ministry to meet the needs of women in your fellowship. He will also use the connection they will inevitably make with other women while creating with their hands and their hearts. They will also heed God's calling to document the stories of God at work in their lives for their families now and for years to come.

I applaud your interest in creating a Women's Scrapbooking Ministry in your church, women's group, or even in your home. Please let us know how Reminders of Faith can continue to support your efforts.

Serving our Glorious Lord,

Sandra L. Joseph

Sandra l. Joseph
President
Reminders Of Faith, Inc

A special thank you to my dear friend,
Carolyn McNicol, for her time and ideas as
this book came together.

"I thank my God everytime I remember you."
Philippians 1:3

What Makes Your Event a "Ministry"

There are many scrapbooking events held by stores and various organizations. Your event will be different as you inspire and teach others to scrapbook God's stories in their lives. Centering your event on God's call to remember His faithfulness to us sets your event apart from an event that only focuses on scrapbooking techniques.

Be sure that you have a clear vision for the purpose of your ministry scrapbooking events. Is it to provide outreach to the community, or to provide fellowship for the women of your congregation? However you answer this question, your scrapbooking event should be unique by centering on a strong spiritual emphasis. There are scrapbooking events held at stores and conventions every weekend, but a women's ministry scrapbooking event will be different in that it will emphasize the importance of passing on your legacy of faith.

One of the best ways to share the importance of the gospel at a scrapbooking event, particularly a larger cropping event, is to have participants share their faith stories through their scrapbook pages. Scrapbooking your faith is not just about placing scripture verses on your layouts, but about actually telling the stories of how God has worked in your life. These scrapbook pages should tell stories of God's salvation in their lives and how they have seen God at work through every day events, such as holiday celebrations and trips to the zoo. Those sharing should be able to articulate their faith as well as provide well-designed scrapbook pages that will appeal to others. Displaying sample layouts also will provide inspiration.

The sharing time should be inspiring and present a clear Gospel message. Always have information packets available that include a booklet about salvation, and encourage those who have questions about God's plan of salvation to leave with these packets. One we can recommend is, *I Want to Go to Heaven When I Die*, written by Woodrow Kroll, and available from Back to the Bible, http://www.backtothebible.org. There are many great materials available that are easily accessible through a bit of research. Include the name of the women's ministry director, the times of your church services, and other programs that may be of interest to women (such as children's programs etc.). The packet should be creatively designed – use your scrapbooking experts to create a tag for the packet to make it visually appealing to those receiving it.

The bookmark and scrapbook page layout pictured above were both created using products and instructions from the *Remember the Wonders* kit pictured on page 30.

How To Get Started: Scrapbooking

Many people are overwhelmed at the thought of sorting through photographs, so they tend to use this as an excuse not to begin. But if you take this process step by step, the seemingly mundane task doesn't have to be daunting, but can actually be enjoyable!

1. Always start with your most recent photos- perhaps even those still waiting to be developed. Get them printed and choose the best ones for your layout(s). Generally, 4 to 6 photos are used on a 2-page layout, but you can also use just one very special photo for a more dramatic effect. Always choose one photo to be your focal point.

2. Choose your scrapbook products to match the theme of the photos. Consider using only 2 or 3 colors that will compliment the colors found in the photos you have chosen to use. Creatively crop and mat your photos and arrange them on the scrapbook page, paying close attention to the direction in which your eye moves. A well-balanced design is a successful one, and your eye should follow effortlessly through the page, rather than bounce around. Once you are pleased with the layout, adhere the elements to your page.

3. Be sure to journal about your thoughts, feelings and experiences. The viewer of the layout should be able to answer the "who," "what," "when," and "where," along with the "why" of the scrapbook layout. Keep in mind that in years to come, those looking at your scrapbook will not be as interested in your artistic layout as the message from your heart, which can only be found in your words.

4. Creative touches such as embellishment tags, pattern papers, die cuts and such can be added as desired. These creative touches should enhance the message of the layout, not become the primary focal point.

5. Remember that not every layout has to be a masterpiece; rather it should tell the story of how God is working in your life.

Layout created using Reminders of Faith™ Love Theme pack.

Planning Your Scrapbook Ministry Event

Planning and executing a scrapbook ministry is different than many other women's ministry events. Always remember that you may have women who will attend a scrapbooking event who would not even consider entering a church for a service or study. Be sure that you plan accordingly with these women in mind.

- **Who to Invite and Where to Find Them:** Any woman who has memories, cherished photos & memorabilia, and a desire to share her life moments with others. The scriptures tell us that Mary treasured all these things in her heart (Luke 2:19 & 51). Women have a God-given desire to store and preserve their precious memories. You will be able to find these women in your church, at MOPS, Bible Studies, Christian Schools and Preschools, and other women's ministries events. Reach out into your communities through newspapers, posters, libraries, grocery stores, doctor's offices, school and athletic events targeting all ages. Don't forget your community of senior citizens when inviting attendees, as they will undoubtedly have a wealth of memories to document. Consider utilizing the Internet where you can post your event on both scrapbooking and women's ministry websites.

- **Length of Event:** The time allotted for a scrapbooking event, including set-up time, should be no less than 3 hours - the most productive scrapbooking event would be between 4 and 5 hours, assuming that not everyone will arrive on time ready to begin. Keep in mind that time should be allowed to provide attendees with the opportunity to set up their scrapbooking supplies, socialize for a brief time, and get into a creative state of mind.

❀ **Time Frame for Evening:**

o   Designate someone to meet and greet people as they enter the building, offering a warm welcome, along with instructions on where to go, how to find a work space, and what the evening ahead will hold. This will allow for a more comfortable transition.

o   First 30 to 45 Minutes – Attendees arrive, set up their workstations, and briefly interact with one another.

o   15 – 20 minutes after the event has begun, the designated hostess should welcome attendants, begin announcements & introductions, and engage in a short devotional of 7 – 10 minutes in duration.

o   Work time – This depends on the time you have allotted for the event.

o   Wrap-up - A great way to end the evening is to provide the opportunity for those who would like to share a scrapbook layout that they created to do so. This should be started approximately 30 to 45 minutes before the end of the event.

o   Ending – Be sure to begin announcing that the event will be coming to a close no later than 30 minutes prior to the event's end. This will provide the opportunity to finish layouts and begin clean-up.

❀ **Room Set-Up:** Each participant will need a minimum of 2 feet of her own space in which to work. You may use either round (5' or 8') or rectangle tables (6' or 8'), both of which have their own benefits, although a round table will require more floor space and will not accommodate as many scrapbookers. However, since defining each scrapbooker's 2 feet of space can be challenging, the round table will allow for better communication between the women attending the event. Round tables are most often used at large cropping events where they are most readily available. Rectangular tables can be used alone or placed together to create a large working space. The biggest drawback to this type of table is that the long surfaces tend to yield a less intimate area for fellowship outside of the participants who are seated directly across from each other. If at all possible, be sure to provide comfortable chairs, as your participants will spend most of their time sitting, arched over the layouts they are working on. It is important to provide enough space between tables and chairs to accommodate wheeled carts filled with scrapbook tools and supplies. If these carts protrude out into the aisles, they become a tripping hazard and possibly even a liability for your venue. Another good tip is to use a carpeted facility whenever possible, which will help to create a warm, inviting atmosphere as well as a great sound absorber. If you do need to use a sound system, always be sure to pre-check the acoustics – a poor sound system can be irritating and distracting to attendees. It is also important to encourage a clutter-free environment by providing a waste container at each table to accommodate scraps of paper, adhesive backing and other disposable items. Use either a plastic trash bag attached to the table or back of the chair, or a plastic bucket-type container in the middle of the table. Your janitorial staff will thank you and your room will have a cleaner appearance, providing a more efficient work environment.

❀ **What tools need to be available:** The only thing you are obligated to provide is the space. While it is wonderful if you are able to provide tool stations with personal die cutting machines, these are not a requirement. Many church children's ministries are using these machines and will often lend them to scrapbook ministries. If you happen to have the budget to purchase them, Die Cutting Machines from Ellison Sizzex™ and Accu-Cut Zip'eCut™ make wonderful tools that can be used for many church ministries. Of course, you will have to choose which dies to provide. The most popular include alphabet, frames, and inspirational shapes. Be sure to ask other scrapbookers to donate tools they no longer use for a basic tool station, and find out whether your attendees would be willing to share their tools during an event.

Another possibility is to ask Scrapbook and Craft stores for donations of tools and products that are either not selling or have been used. Be sure to check with your church to determine if they can provide a tax write-off for these types of items to those donating them. When using tool stations, be clear during your announcements that the tools provided should only be used at the tool station, to avoid participants inadvertently packing them up with their own items. It is always a good to keep an inventory of the tools you provide at your stations.

❀ **Food, Yes or No?** The decision to have food available is optional, but it will make your event more appealing to your attendees. Among the most common refreshments provided are drinks – both hot and cold. The only requirement here should be that all drinks be served in covered containers, as you would not any drinks to spill on someone's scrapbook layout or photos. Any food served should be easy and of the "finger" variety, such as pretzels or M&Ms™ (a favorite of scrapbookers!). Avoid serving food that leaves an oily texture to the hands, such as popcorn or potato chips. Many scrapbookers will bring their own snacks and share them with those at their table. Consider offering a sign-up sheet to encourage your participants to bring different items to share.

❀ **Door Prizes:** If your church allows and provided you have the time, you can request door prize donations from scrapbook manufactures, direct sale consultants, and craft and scrapbook stores. These can be used as drawing giveaways or as prizes for layouts created. However, take care not to present this in a way that your attendees come to expect gifts at every event, or you may find yourself spending most of your time requesting products for giveaways. A great way to organize your requests for door prizes is to send one letter a year asking for products, then distributing what you receive throughout the entire year. Typically, Reminders of Faith is pleased to support Women's Scrapbooking Ministries with bookmarks for each attendee.

🌸 **Wording for Church Bulletin and Bulletin Board Ideas**: "…He commanded our forefathers to teach to their children, so the next generationwould know them, even the children yet to be born, and they in turn would tell their children. Then they would put their trust in God and would not forget His deeds but would keep His commands." Psalm 78:5-7 Scrapbooking provides a wonderful opportunity to share your journey with God. Come and join us on [DATE, TIME, PLACE] to create your own scrapbook. Leave behind a heritage of who you are and what you believe, and offer encouragement for our future generations to put their confidence in God.

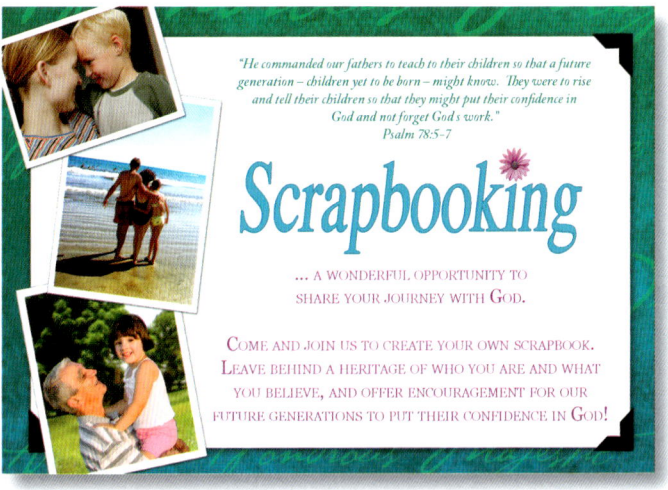

Above is a sample of a postcard that can be sent announcing your your event. A copy of this postcard is on the disk included with this booklet for you to use for your event.

Planning and Executing a Crop

Many women's ministries plan cropping events for fundraisers focused on missionaries' needs, church programs or community needs, or just as a special women's event. Bringing women together for a cropping event is special for attendees if well planned out.

A cropping event is different from your typical scrapbooking event, as this is a large one-day event for a group of scrapbookers to gather to work on their projects. This is large event, generally accommodating between 25 to hundreds of attendees, which typically lasts all day and often into the evening. Because of this, it often requires a great deal more planning and preparation.

- **Allow enough time to effectively plan your crop.** Plan on a minimum of 6 months to prepare for an event of 50 or more.

- **Make a timeline** of what needs to be done, when it needs to be done, and stick to it. Start with choosing your date, facility and event theme. Your timeline will contain such items as the date and content of all event communications, donation & gift requests, meetings for those involved, advanced labor (such as gift bag compilation, name tags, Make & Take projects, etc), outline of events, and on-site set up.

- **Use your theme** for every decision. Your announcements, decorations, food, music, gift bags, and contests should all be created with your theme in mind. Let your creativity flow as you plan your event. The best crops carry a theme that everyone can relate to!

❀ **Your Facility:** Be aware of the facility's space you have chosen to host the event. The minimum space that is needed for an individual participant is two feet. Again, the use of round tables will facilitate conversation and a more intimate fellowship, while rectangular tables will provide scrapbookers with their own defined space. Be sure that everyone is able to see where the MC will be located; it is natural for people to feel left out of a group if they are unable to see all of the activity (see Room Set-Up (pg. 11-12) under Planning your Scrapbook Ministry Event for further details). Be sure that your current insurance policy will provide the coverage needed for this type of event.

Layout created using Reminders of Faith™ Baby Girl theme pack

❀ **Do as much as possible in advance.** Filling gift bags, making name tags, setting up the space, and other jobs from your time line need to be done as early as possible.

- **Plan a detailed outline of the cropping event.** Always create a written outline of the event, including details of who is speaking and when, what contests will be played, what door prizes will be given, and what (if any) companies will be promoted, along with the specific guidelines of each event. Always plan extra contests, door prizes, or Make & Takes, as you won't want to find yourself left with more time than activities.

- **Speak no more than once every half hour, but at least once an hour.** Scrapbookers want to be able to work, but enjoy having fun with fellow participants as well.

- **Make the "rounds" by visiting each table and chatting with your guests.** They will enjoy your hospitality and your interest in their scrapbook pages, and these contacts can serve as wonderful opportunities for sharing.

Layout created using Reminders of Faith™ Legacy theme pack

17

- **Always set the guidelines for the crop at the beginning.** Outline a schedule of events, introduce hostesses and speakers, provide the rules for the tool station, and mention when the major door prizes will be given. This helps set the tone for the event. Here are some common cropping rules:
    - o   No open drinks or no drinks at the table
    - o   Tool Station tools must be utilized at the station
    - o   Be considerate of other's work space
    - o   Seats are intended for croppers, not supplies
    - o   Have a good time!

Christian music provides a nice background, but should not be too loud or too soft. Music will help croppers feel more comfortable in their surroundings and with each other.

- **Always have a back-up plan in case something goes wrong.** Obtain your participants' phone numbers in case you need to cancel your event, and be sure to carry additional door prizes in case you have 2 or more winners. In general, be prepared. Don't be afraid to go the extra mile when compensating for problems that may arise, even if they are not your fault. Never make excuses, but acknowledge mistakes and move on with your event.

- **Make your best give-away gift your last drawing** or contest; this will hold the attention of your audience.

- **Remain happy, positive, and hospitable to the very end!** End the event on a positive note so that your participants will leave knowing that you enjoyed hosting them. They will likely want to come again.

- **Themes for Scrapbook Ministries Crops:** Create your decorations, food, music, gift bags, door prizes, and promotional pieces around the following theme ideas, or better yet, create one of your own!

Sample crop themes listed below, themes in pink have complete instructions on the pages following this list.

Spa Day
Down Home on the Farm (Western)
Birthday
Seasons
Garden Party
Pretty In Pink Party
Come As You Are
Olympics
Picnic
Fairy Tales
Flower Power
Tropical Paradise
Share The Memories Party
Multi Generational Crops
Mother-Daughter
Missions Around the World
Chocolate Lovers
Back to School
Disney
Camp
Crop Hop (50's theme)
Pity and Pamper Me PMS
Sports
Tail Gate Party

Happy Birthday to You

"Rejoice in the Lord always. I will say it again: Rejoice!"
Philippians 4:4
Focus on rejoicing in the life the Lord has given you to live. How precious life is and how it all comes from God.

"I thank my God every time I remember you."
Philippians 1:3
Focus on the thanksgiving you have for the people who birthday's you are celebrating.

Decorations:
- Streamers, Balloons, Party hats and blowers.
- Table Centerpiece: Make each table a different month, ladies have to sit at the table where their birth month is!

January: Mittens, New Year's party stuff, snowmen and snowflakes
February: Valentine's Day- old candy boxes, hearts, roses, President's Day- pictures of presidents
March: Spring- daffodils, lions and lambs, St. Patrick's Day- green shamrocks and Irish hats
April: Easter- bunnies, eggs, baskets, Showers- umbrellas
May: Silk Flowers, Mother's Day- figurines, old cards, poems, Mom books, Memorial Day- flags
June: Father's Day- old cards, tools, ties, Weddings- Bridal Magazines, bells, and lace
July: 4th- flags, confetti, red, white and blue
August: picnics, vacations- maps, brochures, seashells, travel games
September: Back to School- plaid, books, pencils, crayons, school supplies
October: Harvest: pumpkins, candy corn, apples,
November: Thanksgiving- cornucopia, gourds, pilgrims, Indians, turkeys
December: Christmas- decorations, presents, and Santa Claus.

Music:
- Happy Birthday Album...$6.98 (CD available at Amazon.com)

Contests:
- Oldest, youngest, closest birthday to event, same birthday.
- Blindfold contest: put candles on a cake
- Table contest: without talking, stand in order from youngest to oldest or put birthdays in order

Gift Bags:
- Birthday Scrapbooking Supplies

Food:
- Birthday Cake
- Cupcakes with Candles

Chocolate Lovers

"They are sweeter than honey, than honey from the comb."
Psalm 19: 7- 10, featuring verse 10b

Focus on how chocolate may satisfy your craving for sweets but God's words and his ways provide a sweetness that never needs fed again.

Decorations:
      Candy Bar wrappers, Chocolate Cookbooks, Containers of Coco, Hot Chocolate, Chocolate-scented candles or soap.

Food:
- Chocolate Covered Pretzels
- M&M's
- Hershey's Miniatures
- Hot chocolate or chocolate milk
- Fudge

Contests:
- Name all the colors of M&M (go to www.mms.com ~as of printing there were 21)
- Tape different candy wrappers under seats for door prizes
- Trivia contest about information concerning chocolate (Do you know the first name of Mr. Hershey? Answer: Milton)
- Play Chocolate Bingo with names of different candy bars

Door Prize:
- 1 pound chocolate bar or other kinds of chocolates

Camp

"O Lord, our Lord, how majestic is your name in all the earth."
Psalm 8:1
Focus on the absolute beauty and wonder of God's creation.

Decorations:
- Camp Items- bandannas, flashlights, acorns, camping guides, camping supplies, sleeping bag
- Set up a tent for people to get their picture taken in
- Spread Pine fresheners around the room to make it smell like the woods

Music:
- "Favorite Camp Songs"…$5.49 (CD's available at Amazon.com)

Food:
- Smores
- Trail mix
- Hot chocolate

Contests:
- Singing Camp Songs contest
- Hide bugs underneath some peoples chairs
- Mad Libs
- Give out the following award for each camper:
    - Cleanest Cropping Area
    - Most Pages
    - Least Pages
    - Camp Spirit
    - Early Bird

Gift Bags:
- Bug spray
- Autograph book for camp friends autographs
- Camping scrapbooking items

Teaching a Class on Scrapbooking Your Faith

Teaching a class on how to scrapbook your faith is an excellent opportunity to motivate others to leave behind the stories of God's faithfulness in their lives. You can teach a class like this at your church, a women's event, craft and scrapbook stores, scrapbook events such as conventions and crops, women's retreats, and even as part of your scrapbook women's ministry program.

- **Classroom:** Once again, be sure that each student has adequate space. Request that the room be set in a classroom setting, meaning that there are tables in front with chairs behind.

- **Class outline:** List your class objectives, what products will be used, and outline what projects will be created. Typically a class will run 1 1/2 – 2 hours long and will involve a 1-2 scrapbook page layout and a tag or card. A class on scrapbooking your faith should be designed for a beginner's level.

- **Class Presentation:** Since scrapbooking is a visual craft, your students will learn best by being able to see step-by-step what they are to do next. Classes should be presented by utilizing visual tools, such as overhead projectors or Power Point presentations.

- **Class Kits:** All materials used in the Scrapbooking Your Faith classes should be packaged in a kit for the students. Provide a copy of the finished product in case some do not finish it on time. Be sure to leave yourself enough time to compile the kits before the class begins.

Sample Reminders of Faith Class outline

Class Objective: To inspire and teach the student how to document her faith through scrapbooking their photos, memorabilia, thoughts, and memories.

Scripture Encouragement: Remembering What God Has Done

In Joshua 4, when the Lord opened the Jordan River for the Israelites to cross, He told them to build a monument from the river stones. The Lord knew that their children would ask, "What do these stones mean?" They were to respond by sharing God's faithfulness to bring them to the promise land. This monument served as a reminder to them and their future generations of what God has done.

We, too, are called to leave reminders of God's faithfulness.

"...He commanded our forefathers to teach to their children, so the next generation would know them, even the children yet to be born, and they in turn would tell their children. Then they would put their trust in God and would not forget his deeds but would keep his Commands." Psalm 78:5-7

Scrapbooking provides a wonderful opportunity to share your journey with God. Birthday photos signify another year of God's blessings; landscape photos show God's majesty in His Creation; everyday life photos reveal how God provides without our help.

Our scrapbooks will leave behind a heritage of who we are and what we believe, and offer encouragement for future generations to put their confidence in God.

Both layouts and the card on the following page were created using the papers shown to the left, which include 2 sheets of card stock, 3 pieces of patterned paper, a sheet of vellum imprinted with scripture and imprinted tag embellishment sheets. The only tools required are a paper trimmer, X-Acto knife, and adhesive. A small triange or t-square is most helpful in making straight cuts if you don't have a paper trimmer.

24

Both photos were matted using the Royal Prism paper. Photos were then adhered to the paper and trimed with a ¼ inch border.

An X-Acto knife was used to cut a semi-circle around the button on the tag and the word "Prayer" was tucked underneath.

* see included CD for complete step by step instructions.

The large leaf was cut out and placed on top of strips of the Royal Prism paper.

The same X-Acto knife technique as above was used on the Pray tag.

The border from the tag sheet was torn along one side, then positioned around the verse, adhered to top and bottom. The paper trimmer was used to square off the sides. The entire piece was then mounted on the Emerald paper, and adhered to a card.

25

Using Reminders of Faith Theme Packs at Your Scrapbook Ministry Event

Reminders of Faith theme packs provide creatively designed scripture-based embellishment tags, as well as scripture vellum along with patterned paper and card stock to create layouts of God's faithfulness in your life. Each theme pack has scrapbook layout and card examples on the back, an inspiring message about the theme, and journaling questions to help get your thoughts and memories recorded.

Pictured above is the back of a **Reminders of Faith Theme Pack**, pictured to the right are the fronts of the packs.

How to use Reminders of Faith theme packs:

Start with an icebreaker. Have those who are willing share a photo or memorabilia on the evening's theme, but avoid coercing anyone to share if they seem to be uncomfortable. The leader should be prepared to share if no one else is willing. Ask them to describe what the photo or memorabilia is about and how they feel when they remember the situation surrounding the photo.

Give a 7 – 10 minute devotion. Use the write up on the back of the theme pack to create a short devotional on the theme. Use one of the verses from the scripture vellum included in the pack as the theme verse for the evening. Share an experience of your own to make this devotional more personal.

Review the questions on the back of packet. Point out the journaling questions on the back of the theme packs to help participants record their thoughts and memories.

Wrap up and sharing of their page time. Give your participants the opportunity to share their layouts and memories at the end of the evening. Create an environment that will allow for sharing regardless of creative styles, as the women will learn about each other and what God is doing in their lives through their sharing. Close in prayer.

Reminders of Faith Theme Packs for the Year:
September - Faith
October - Prayer
November - Blessing
December - Friendship
January - Peace
February - Love
March - Hope
April - Legacy
May – Mother
June - Creation
July - Family
August – Baby Boy/Baby Girl

27

Using Reminders of Faith, *Remember the Wonders* kits at your Scrapbook Ministy Event

Reminders of Faith's monthly *Remember the Wonders* Scrapbook Kits are sent directly in bulk to groups or to individual subscribers. Unlike theme packs, each kit is designed around a scriptural devotional message, which can be used for the theme of your scrapbook group. The monthly devotional uses Biblical examples to encourage the scrapbooker to reflect on the memories of how God has been faithful to them and then to scrapbook that memory.

The monthly kits contain a full-color, 4 page newsletter featuring an inspiring scriptural message and project photographs with simple instructions on how to recreate the projects shown. Inside the kit will be everything needed to duplicate the samples shown, including embellishment tags, scripture vellum, patterned paper, reversible card stock, fibers, die-cuts and other items. The newsletter will also include a special section with ideas on simple cards and other paper crafts to help share your faith and encourage one another.

How to use *Remember the Wonders* Kits:

Start your evening with a small icebreaker. Be sure that everyone is introduced and consider having those present share a photo they intend to document at this event.

Immediately give a 7 - 10 minute devotional. Using the spiritual theme from the newsletter devotional, read the scripture reference and share how God has used this scripture in your life. Make one of the projects from the *Remember the Wonders* newsletter and material to share with the group. Showing how you have put these ideas to work for you is a tremendous visual help to your attendees.

Pick one of the featured projects from the newsletter to encourage the group to create. *Remember the Wonders* packs come complete with everything needed to create scrapbook layouts and other paper craft projects such as cards, small albums, and tags. It may be fun for your group to spend an evening creating cards or even a small tribute album.

Be sure to have copies of the the Newsletter featured on each table. Since one of the highlights of the *Remember the Wonders* packs is photographs of already-completed projects, be sure to have these examples on each table for view. Even though attendees will add their own touches, having the sample in front of them will help get them started.

The card and Journal pictured above were both created using products and instructions from the *Remember the Wonders* kit pictured on page 30.

29

Wrap-up and sharing of their creations. Come together at the end of the evening to share what has been created and how working on the *Remember the Wonders* spiritual theme has reminded your attendees of what God has done or is doing in their lives. Create an accepting environment by encouraging each person, and find something to compliment them on -- their journaling, use of scripture, or even how their heart's message was revealed in their work. Do remember that this sharing time will allow your group to grow in learning more about each other and may open their hearts to a greater understanding of God's work in their lives.

Close the event in prayer, thanking God for the opportunity to remember what He has done in our lives.

Pictured above are the contents of a *Remember the Wonders* Kit, including patterned paper, card stock, scripture vellum, tag embellishment sheet, die cut title, alphabet stickers, buttons, charms and three yards of fibers.
Not shown are the blank journal and newsletter.

Basic Scrapbook Information
How To Get Started, Terms and Techniques, etc.

Scrapbooking: The art of creating a scrapbook which records your memories, photos and memorabilia, family traditions, vacations, and other important and cherished events. Scrapbooks are intended to become family heirlooms that will be passed down to future generations.

Photo Safe: Products that are acid-free and lignin-free, meaning that these products are made with a neutral ph that should prevent deterioration of your scrapbook layouts over time.

Layout: The term used to describe any of one or more scrapbook pages created.

Crop: 1. A scrapbook event in which scrapbookers come together to work on their scrapbook projects; 2. To remove unwanted objects from photos by cutting with scissors or using a computer program.

Album: A book in which the created scrapbook layouts are stored and preserved. The most common size is 12 x 12, but also popular are 8 1/2 x 11 or 10 X 10 sized albums. Albums are typically available in the form of 3 ring binders, strap hinge, or post bound top loading styles.

Theme Albums: Scrapbook albums created around a theme such as vacations, holidays or a person's life.

Chronological Albums: Scrapbooks created in sequential order by date.

Scrapbook Tools: Includes such items as scissors, paper trimmers, acid-free pens, photo safe adhesives (i.e. Xyron™, Glue Dots™, etc.), personal die cutting machines (i.e. Sizzex™ and Accu-Cut™), and punches.

Scrapbook Supplies: Includes Pattern Paper, Embellishments, Tags, Die Cuts, Stickers, Card Stock, and other decorative implements.

Layout above and card below were created using materials included in the *Remember the Wonders* kit shown on page 30.

32

Frequently asked questions

🌸 **Where can I find Reminders of Faith products?** Reminders of Faith products can be found at Christian and Scrapbook stores across the United States, as well as online. Please check our website at **www.remindersoffaith.com/stores.php** for a listing of scrapbooking stores that carry our products. Reminders of Faith will also sell to church groups at a 25% discount off of retail, in 25-pack groups (individual papers) or theme packs. The Church tax ID certificate must be provided to us. Please contact us at: **sales@remindersoffaith.com** for more information.

🌸 **How can I teach for Reminders of Faith at other church events?** If you are interested in teaching a Reminders of Faith class at your church or scrapbook event, please contact us at, **teach@remindersoffaith.com**. We welcome the teaching of our classes at church and scrapbook events provided that our product is available to purchase at the event and that our class outline is followed.

🌸 **Where can I find ideas for layouts?** The Reminders of Faith website **www.remindersoffaith.com** has a gallery full of ideas for layouts and cards.

🌸 **What if I plan an event and no one comes?** Even though this is discouraging, remember that God is in control of our events. Don't give up if you truly feel that you are being called to this ministry. Promotion is the key element – if your turnout isn't what you expected, look again at how you can promote your event. The most important step is to pray that God will bring those whom He would desire to your event.

🌸 **Should I allow products to be sold at our event?** If your event is held at the church, this will depend upon what their policies allow, so be sure to get approval for this with your church board ahead of time. If you are not allowed to sell items at your events, set up a swap table and encourage women to purchase items before the event.

🌸 **How should I handle all the different Direct Sale Consultants at our ministry event?** Many women sell scrapbook products through different direct sale companies. Welcome these ladies to your event and if allowed, announce who they are and what companies they represent. In this introduction, encourage women who are interested in making contact with them and arrange a time and place to discuss their products. They should not push attendees to hold or attend a workshop, nor should they add anyone's name to a mailing or email list without a participant's knowledge or consent. Putting your policies in writing will make them clear for direct sale consultants and, as a result, will make everyone involved more comfortable.

🌸 **What if an attendee wants to know more about God and His Salvation after an event?** It is Reminders of Faith's desire that as attendees come to your women's ministry scrapbooking events, they would desire to learn more about God and His gift of Salvation. At the very least, always have information packets available that include a booklet about salvation. Again, *I Want to Go to Heaven When I Die*, written by Woodrow Kroll, available from Back to the Bible, is a great resource. Of course, you can always offer to answer questions directly or have someone at the event willing to answer questions for you if you are not comfortable doing so. Most importantly is to pray for those attending your event that the Lord would continue to work in their lives.

Other Paper Crafting Projects for Scrapbook Ministries

- **Card Fellowships:** Coming together to create cards is the purpose of this group. Using the same tools as the scrapbooking group, this group may also use stamping tools to create cards. The cards are then used to encourage and support others.

- **Tribute Albums:** These albums are created for teachers, pastors, parents, or anyone you want to honor as a group or an individual.

- **History Album:** This album is created to remember what God has done through a church or an organization.

- **Recipe Books:** Use scrapbooking techniques and tools to create a recipe book. This book can include recipes of those attending your group, or you can accept recipes from others. The book created can be done so as a special gift for one particular person (such as your pastor's wife or a special speaker), or it can be duplicated for many others through a print center. You can also use this idea for the new brides or college graduates in your congregation. Be sure that if there is a special recipe submitted by anyone in your church that you create a special page to highlight them and their recipes.

- **Short Term Mission Trip Albums:** Invite the short term missionary groups and/or the families of those who went on the mission trips to come together to create an album of their trip. This is also a wonderful time for the group to share their photographs and memories of the trip.

- **Missionary Books:** Missionary families enjoy the same celebrations throughout the year as we do on birthdays, school memories, vacations, friends and such - but they often don't have the scrapbooking material available to them to document those memories. Come together to create pre-made scrapbook pages (where all that is needed is the photographs) and send to the missionaries, documenting their family memories as well as their mission work. Another great idea is to have a collection of scrapbook materials that can be donated and sent to missionaries so that they can work on their own books. This works well if you ask for supplies to make a double-page layout so that you don't receive a random sheet of stickers. If you choose to use this idea, be sure to supplement the donated supplies with scrapbook necessities such as adhesive, albums, cardstock and additional items that will match what has been donated. Just imagine how appreciative those receiving this gift will be, as it will help them record how God has been working in their lives.

To learn more about Reminders of Faith visit:
www.remindersoffaith.com
To learn more about *Remember the Wonders* kits visit:
www.rememberthewonders.com
To contact Sandra Joseph for speaking events:
sandraj@remindersoffaith.com
To contact Kathy Brundage for Reminders of Faith business:
kathyb@remindersoffaith.com
To order Reminders of Faith products, contact us us at:
orders@remindersoffaith.com

518 Overhead Drive,
Moon Township, PA 15108
412-720-2699

Our Mission

The mission of Reminders Of Faith is to teach people to remember God's Faithfulness throughout their lives. We will serve God as a Christian Publishing, Consulting, Product Design, and Event Company. Reminders Of Faith will promote the message of God's faithfulness and salvation. Every area of the business will be run with a standard of excellence.

Incorporated in July 2003, Reminders Of Faith, Inc was started to encourage people to tell the stories of God's faithfulness in their lives. President, Sandra Joseph, has had a long career in the scrapbook industry including the founding National Director of Memories Community and the conceptional analyst for Memories Expo. Starting in 1999, Sandra felt the Lord's call on her life to inspire women not just to make beautiful scrapbook pages, but to tell the stories of God's faithfulness in their lives. Walking away from a book deal in 2002 because she was asked to soften the gospel message, she continued to feel the Lord's call on her life to remember what God has done. The Lord brought together Sandra and Kathy Brundage, to bring the Reminders Of Faith concept to actuality. Kathy's gifts in technology and her business background brought Reminders Of Faith's books and products to the marketplace. Releasing their first book, Scrapbooking Your Spiritual Journey, by Sandra, and related products in February 2004, the company has experienced God's blessing in both the Scrapbooking and Christian marketplace. Responding to consumer demands, *Remember the Wonders* kits were developed. As we continue on our journey we pray that we will be faithful to God's calling. We hope that our books and products will provide the opportunity for you to tell the stories of God's faithfulness in your lives. This is our prayer for your family, our families and for all of our future generations.

Other books by Reminders of Faith

Scrapbooking Your Spiritual Journey
Inspiring you to tell the stories of God's faithfulness to future generations.
By Sandra L. Joseph

Through her personal stories and scrapbook pages, Sandra L. Joseph inspires and motivates others to scrapbook the stories of God's faithfulness in their lives.

Passing On Your Legacy Of Love
Scrapbooking with a Purpose.
By Marci Whitford

Marci has written an invaluable and heartfelt book about creating a scrapbook about one of the most significant people in history - you. She inspires her readers to leave a priceless gift that will one day be left to your loved ones.

Reflections on God's Wonders
Scrapbooking God's Creation in the World Around You.
By Allison Collins

Allison shares her testimony and heartfelt feelings on the pages of her scrapbook as she recognizes God's handprint in the world around her. She shows how your photos of nature can be a reflection of God. A valuable resouce for those who love to travel.

Reminding future generations of God's faithfulness!

Reminders of Faith books and products can be found at Christian bookstores and craft stores everywhere.
See our website for a listing of stores that carry our products.

Please ask your local Christian store about ordering information!

Remember The Wonders Church Group Order Form

518 Overhead Drive   Info: 412-720-2699
Moon Township, PA 15108   Fax: 412-264-7857
www.remindersoffaith.com   Email: orders@rememberthewonders.com

Qty	Product Name	Product		Price each	25% Dis-
	Monthly Club Kit	Specify Month below	retail price	1-10 kits	10 or more kits
	Monthly kit group order		34.95	29.95	24.95

All papers are true 12x12, acid free & lignin free

Church:
Phone: P.O. #
Email: Tax ID #
Billing Address:
City, State Zip

Included on the CD

An eye-catching, full color post card invitation to your event. Your information can be added on the blank back.

❀

A full page and half page bulletin insert advertisement in black and white and full color.

❀

A complete class outline.

❀

Step-by-step full color samples of a project in .jpg format for your personal instruction or to add to a power point presentation

❀

Written step-by-step instuctions to complete the same project.

❀

A CD should be attached to the inside back cover. Please contact us if yours does not contain one or if you need to order a replacement.